Studies In Jainism:

Reader 1

Edited by

Duli Chandra Jain

Jain Study Circle

Editorial Advisors:

Jyotiben R. Gandhi
Vinay K. Vakani

Cover:
Interior views of Delwara Jain Temples
Mt. Abu, Rajasthan, India
Photos by DCJ

Copyright © 1990 Jain Study Circle, Inc.

Library of Congress Catalog Card No. 90 - 091543

ISBN   0 - 9626105 - 0 - X   Softcover

Published by
Jain Study Circle, Inc.
99-11 60 Avenue, #3D
Flushing, New York, 11368
USA

Printed in the United States of America

Dedicated to

The New Generation Of Jains

Contents

Preface

These are exciting times for Jainism. For the first time in recorded history, a significant population of Jains is residing outside of India. We are living in the age of science and technology, computers and communication satellites, and rockets and space exploration. All over the world, the political and socio-economic systems are undergoing important changes. With the dawn of freedom and democracy, which some of us have personally witnessed, India has made significant progress in the past few decades in various fields including agriculture, industry and education. Indians who have migrated to North America, including youngsters, have made excellent use of the opportunities presented to them. Jains are no exception.

In India as well as in North America, Jains are playing a significant role in several diverse fields and are enjoying the benefits of their endeavors. There has been a significant rise in the level of education in the Jain community. Consequently, Jains have achieved greater awareness and understanding of the basics of religion. They have developed the ability to distinguish between blind faith and rationalism, between myths and reality, and between meaningless rituals and the genuine practice of religion. A healthy dialogue is continuing on the unique features of Jainism. This book is a modest effort to contribute to such dialogue.

The concepts presented in the book conform to the Jain scriptures which are works of great

i

thinkers and philosophers of the past. Every effort has been made to avoid views and interpretations of scriptures given by individual preachers and writers. Earlier chapters in the book mostly present the Jain concept of reality while the latter chapters contain the code of conduct. The code of ethics of all religions including Jainism, is essentially the same. However, the Jain code of conduct is based on our concepts of universe and of reality. Moreover, Jains practice ethical conduct not because some higher authority commands them to do so. They do not celebrate any worship to please any superhuman or supernatural being. Jains conduct their lives in a rational manner in order to attain happiness and peace of mind individually as well as collectively.

The present work is the result of the joint effort of a large group of individuals. Most of the material has been adopted from the Jain Study Circular. Thus, the writers of the Jain Study Circular should be given the most credit for their contributions. As advisors, Dr. Jyotiben R. Gandhi and Mr. Vinay K. Vakani have made valuable comments and suggestions. Our youngsters, Ahamindra Jain, Vineesh Jain, Alpa, Sangeeta and Vipul Sanghvi, Dr. Anuja Shah, Asha Shah and Prerna Shah, have helped in editing the manuscript. Many friends, Mr. Atul Jain, Dr. T. J. Salgia, Mr. Naresh Shah and others, have provided advice and guidance. I am also grateful for the advice, encouragement and help given by Dr. Chaman Lal Jain, Dr. Rajendra K. Jain, Mr. Pravin K. Shah and my wife, Sunita.

D.C.J.

NAMOKAAR MANTRA
(REVERENCE MANTRA)

NAMO ARIHANTAANAM
We revere the Supreme Human Beings (ARIHANTs) because they achieve absolute truth and devote their lives for the uplift of life on earth.

NAMO SIDDHAANAM
We revere the Supreme Beings (SIDDHAs) because they are souls having absolute perception, knowledge and bliss.

NAMO AAYIRIYAANAM
We revere the Sages who preach (ACHARYAs) because they master the principles of religion.

NAMO UVAJJHAAYAANAM
We revere the Sages who study (UPAADHYAAYAs) because they engage in enhancing their knowledge of matter and souls.

NAMO LOAE SAVVA SAAHOONAM
We revere all Sages (SADHUs) because they devote their lives to selfless pursuit of the enlightenment of all.

We revere them with a determination to follow in their footsteps and make our lives more meaningful.

② Five Supreme Benevolent Personalities (PANCH PARAMESHTHI)

We Jains pray to and worship five supreme benevolent personalities. They are our ideals. We worship their virtues. The five supreme benevolent personalities are:

ARIHANTs are supreme human beings who enjoy absolute perception, knowledge and bliss. The word ARAHANT is Prakrit for the Sanskrit word ARHAT which means one who is worthy of respect. A variation of ARAHANT is ARIHANT which means one who has conquered his inner enemies (passions). ARIHANTs do not have any likes or dislikes for any person, material or creed. They are beyond attachment and aversion (VEETARAAG). ARIHANTs are omniscient (KEVALI). They know the absolute truth about souls and universe. ARIHANTs devote their entire lives for the uplift of life on earth. At the end of their lives, they become pure souls (SIDDHAs) and attain salvation (NIRVANA).

SIDDHAs are liberated souls that do not have any kind of attachment with other substances of the universe. A worldly soul becomes liberated and attains salvation by shedding all karma particles in its possession. SIDDHAs do not interfere in the affairs of the universe. They enjoy the qualities of a pure soul, infinite perception, knowledge and bliss.

ACHARYAs are monks who know the principles of religion. They strictly follow the teachings of religion. They give up passions such as anger, pride, ego, intrigue (deceit) and greed. They are the role models for other monks as well as for householders.

UPAADHYAAYAs are monks who study and research the scriptures. On mastering the scriptural knowledge, they become Acharyas.

SADHUs are monks who follow the path to spiritual progress. The monks take the five great vows of nonviolence (AHIMSA), truth (SATYA), non-stealing (ACHAURYA), celibacy (BRAHMACHARYA) and non-possessiveness (APARIGRAH). Their daily routine consists of study of scriptures and meditation about the principles of the Jain religion. The life of a monk is the ideal which every householder hopes to achieve. In this manner, a monk performs a great service to society.

In Jainism, the word 'OM' is the symbol for the five supreme benevolent personalities. It is a combination of the following letters:

A for ARIHANT
A for ASHAREERI (one who is without a body, SIDDHA)
A for ACHARYA
U for UPAADHYAAYA
M for MUNI (monk, SADHU)

We remember the pristine qualities of all supreme benevolent personalities while saying the word 'OM'.

In NAMOKAAR Mantra, we pray to these five supreme benevolent personalities. Although, SIDDHAs are spiritually higher than ARIHANTs, we pray to ARIHANTs first because they show us the path to liberation. We should bear in mind that the five supreme benevolent personalities do not grant us any favors. They are the ideals for us to follow.

Jain Religion

The Sanskrit word for religion is 'DHARM' meaning the nature of things. Thus qualities or virtues of a human being constitute his/her religion. Another meaning of the word 'DHARM' is duty. Religion teaches us to do our duties well.

The word Jain is derived from the Sanskrit word 'JIN' which means victor, the individual who has conquered his passions such as anger, pride, intrigue and greed. The followers of 'JIN' are called Jains and the religion followed by them is the Jain religion. ARIHANTs are JINs. They as well as SIDDHAs are omniscient. They know the absolute truth about souls and the universe.

The omniscient gave the knowledge about souls, matter and other things and events of the universe to their followers. The scholarly monks (Acharyas) composed a number of scriptures based on such knowledge. These scriptures were handed down by word of mouth from one generation to the next for a few hundred years. Later the scriptures were put into writing and more scriptures were written. Thus Jains have a wealth of scriptural knowledge available to them. We Jains are expected to study these scriptures and understand the basic concepts of soul, matter and other entities of the universe.

In ancient times, the followers of Jain religion were called SHRAMANs or NIRGRANTHs. SHRAMAN is one who is self-reliant, one who believes in self-help for one's own improvement and progress. NIRGRANTH is one who does not blindly accept what is written in any religious book. NIRGRANTHs believe that the absolute truth can not be written or spoken in words. The absolute truth is known to omniscient (KEVALI) only. We Jains study the scriptures and accept what seems appropriate according to our understanding and experience.

The word NIRGRANTH also means one who does not have any anxiety. NIRGRANTHs do not have any anxiety about physical pleasures and pains because they understand that these are the realities of life. We have pleasures and pains as a result of the laws of nature which apply to all the things and events in the universe. In other words, NIRGRANTHs do not experience the anxiety associated with physical pleasures and pains because they realize and accept the fact that these features are an integral and inseparable part of life.

The purpose of religion is to improve life on earth. Religion helps us maintain good physical and mental health, both individually and collectively. Thus religion is the science of living. The Jain religion helps us live a better life and have peace of mind. It teaches that men and women of all races and religions are equal. It promotes harmony and peace in society.

We, the followers of the Jain religion, have the basic concepts given below:

1. We Jains are the followers of NIRGRANTHS. Therefore, we do not accept what is written in any religious books without proper understanding. We Jains need not believe in anything which does not appeal to our common sense. We do not believe that any superhuman or

supernatural power created the universe or controls it. No supernatural power rewards us for our good deeds or punishes us for our bad deeds. All things and events in the universe take place because of the laws of nature. It implies that all living beings of the universe are independent. We know that pleasures and pains are part of life. So we accept them without undue concern.

2. We Jains are the followers of SHRAMANS. Thus we believe in self-help. We believe that we are the masters of our destiny. We Jains do not pray to God for favors. We do not pray to any gods (DEVs) and goddesses (DEVIs) for favors. We also believe that a religious act such as prayer, worship and fasting should be performed with pure thoughts and feelings. Otherwise, these religious practices do not lead to our spiritual progress.

In conclusion, we Jains believe in self-help. We understand that pains and pleasures are part of our worldly existence. We understand that TEERTHANKARS, ARIHANTS and SIDDHAS do not give us any reward or punishment. We pray to VEETARAAG JIN and worship their virtues of absolute perception, absolute knowledge and non-attachment. We pray and worship with the intention of imbibing the virtues of VEETARAAG JIN.

JIN, JIN, BLESS HIS NAME
by Mrs. Leona Smith Kremser

Children, hear your elders talking to you,
When the food is not pure vegetarian food,
JIN, JIN, remember His name.

Sons, hear your fathers talking to you,
When the earning is not fair and honest,
JIN, JIN, remember His name.

Daughters, hear your mothers talking to you,
When the love is nothing but physical, lust,
JIN, JIN, remember His name.

His right perception to guide you;
His right knowledge to enrich you;
His right conduct to nourish you;
In the tempting hour upon you.

Then you call His name.
Then your religion is your guidepost,
And your new land is your bright unfoldment.
. . . . JIN, JIN, bless His name.

In this poem, the word JIN refers to all omniscients
(KEVALIs).

Twenty-Four TEERTHANKARS

According to Jain philosophy, the universe has no beginning and no end. Similarly, the Jain religion was not started by any individual or group. It is eternal. The principles of Jainism have always been in existence.

The word TEERTHANKAR is derived from the Sanskrit word TEERTH which means religious order. One who reinstates the religious order is called TEERTHANKAR. The basic principles of Jainism remain unchanged. However, Jains believe that as time passes, people lose sight of the true spirit of religion and adopt some undesirable practices. Also, our religious practices need reform and modification as times and circumstances change. TEERTHANKARS are religious personalities who reform and modify the Jain religious system. They perform penance (TAPAH) and meditate upon the nature of soul and its place in the universe. They give up all attachment (RAAG) and aversion (DWESH). Thus they become VEETARAAG which means beyond attachment (likes) and aversion (dislikes). They become omniscient (KEVALI). By practicing religion in its true spirit, they teach the principles of religion to their followers. They reform and modify the religious system according to the conditions that exist during their times. In the end, they perform pristine meditation (SHUKLA DHYAAN) and attain NIRVANA. TEERTHANKARS are ARIHANTS. TEERTHANKARS are also called JINENDRA or

JINESHWAR. Bhagwaan, Swami and Prabhu are the titles used with the names of TEERTHANKARS.

Since time immemorial, TEERTHANKARS have been reinstating and modifying the Jain religious system. Twenty-four TEERTHANKARS have lived during the present epoch (half-cycle of time).

Jains worship the images of TEERTHANKARS as reminders of the beautiful principles of the Jain religion. Such prayers and worships give us peace of mind and help us in our spiritual progress. Each TEERTHANKAR's image has an emblem (LAANCHHAN). The emblems help people knowing different languages and scripts recognize the images. The names of the twenty-four TEERTHANKARS and the emblems of their images are:

Twenty-Four TEERTHANKARS And Their Emblems

TEERTHANKAR	Emblem
1. Rishabhadev (Aadinath)	Bullock
2. Ajitnath	Elephant
3. Sambhavanath	Horse
4. Abhinandan	Monkey
5. Sumatinath	Ruddy goose (or curlew)
6. Padmaprabh	Red lotus
7. Supaarshvanath	Swastik
8. Chandraprabh	Crescent
9. Pushpadant (Suvidhinath)	Crocodile
10. Sheetalnath	Wish-yielding tree (or SHREEVATSA)
11. Shreyaansnath	Rhinoceros

12. Vaasupoojya	Buffalo
13. Vimalnath	Boar
14. Anantnath	Porcupine
	(or falcon)
15. Dharmnath	Thunderbolt
	(VAJRA)
16. Shantinath	Deer
17. Kunthunath	He-goat
18. Aranath	Fish
	(or NANDYAVART)
19. Mallinath	Water-pot
20. Munisuvrat	Tortoise
21. Naminath	Blue lotus
22. Neminath	Conch shell
23. Parshvanath	Serpent
24. Mahaveer (Vardhamaan)	Lion

Bhagwaan Mahaveer is the last TEERTHANKAR of the present epoch. Thus we are enjoying the TEERTH or the religious order of Bhagwaan Mahaveer.

* * * * * * *

Truth can not be attained by reason only without practical moral discipline of passions and prejudices which warp human judgement.   - Dr. Ratan Kumar Jain
* * * * * * *

Bhagwaan Mahaveer

Bhagwaan Mahaveer is the twenty-fourth TEERTHANKAR of the present epoch of Jainism. He was born in 599 B.C. at Kshatriyakund to King Siddhaarth and Queen Trishala. Mahaveer was a contemporary of Bhagwaan Buddha, the founder of Buddhism. His parents were followers of Bhagwaan Parshvanath, the twenty-third TEERTHANKAR of Jains.

When Queen Trishala was expecting the baby, she had many beautiful dreams. She asked some scholars about the dreams. They said that she was going to have an extraordinary child, one who will show the path to true happiness to humanity. The child was given the name Vardhmaan which means one who brings prosperity.

There are many stories of Mahaveer's boyhood. They illustrate that from early childhood, Mahaveer believed in practicing nonviolence. He did not use force to control even wild and dangerous animals. He knew that all living beings understand the language of love. Once young Mahaveer was playing with his friends when a snake appeared. His friends were scared and they ran away. However, Mahaveer remained calm and did not disturb the snake. In a little while, the snake went away. On another occasion, Mahaveer was not scared of an elephant who was acting up. The elephant eventually became calm and docile. When people realized Vardhmaan's power of love, they gave him the name Mahaveer, the Great Hero.

Mahaveer lived a life of comfort and luxury. Still he would think of those who were less fortunate than him. He was sensitive to the pain and sufferings of humanity. So he decided to leave home and become a monk. He sought the permission of his elder brother Nandivardhan. Because of his love for Mahaveer, Nandivardhan felt very sad. He could not utter a single word and just sat there with tears in his eyes. Mahaveer understood his brother's feelings and did not leave home at that time.

Later, at the age of thirty, Mahaveer gave up his worldly possessions including all means of comfort. He became a monk and left home. He learned to survive on small amounts of food and reduced his physical needs. He had no anger, pride or desires. He practiced nonviolence, truth and celibacy. He did not take anything including food and water unless it was offered to him. He performed difficult penance, internal as well as physical. He pondered over soul and matter and other entities of the universe. He performed severe penance and meditation for twelve years. In this manner, he rid his soul of four types of karma that obstruct proper perception and knowledge. Mahaveer attained absolute knowledge (KEVAL JNAAN) and became an omniscient. He became VEETARAAG, one who is beyond attachment and aversion. Mahaveer attained the status of JIN, the victor, and of ARIHANT, one who is worthy of respect. We Jains worship these qualities of a supreme human being with the intention of attaining similar qualities.

Bhagwaan Mahaveer discussed the principles of

religion with many scholars of his time including Indrabhooti Gautam. They were greatly influenced by his perception, knowledge and conduct. They became his disciples. Gautam Swami became his principal disciple (GANADHAR). Bhagwaan Mahaveer practiced religion in its true spirit. Remember, the meaning of the Sanskrit word DHARM is attributes or qualities. Bhagwaan Mahaveer enjoyed the attributes of his pure soul. His disciples (GANADHARs) explained the principles of religion to all. They also composed the scriptures which were orally passed on from one generation to the next and were later put into writing. It should be noted that Mahaveer did not start any new religion, he only revived the religion which was earlier preached by other TEERTHANKARs.

Bhagwaan Mahaveer, like other TEERTHANKARs, reformed and modified the religious practices that were going on during his times. Bhagwaan Parshvanath had taught four vows, namely, nonviolence (AHIMSA), truth (SATYA), non-stealing (ACHAURYA) and non-possessiveness (APARIGRAH). Bhagwaan Mahaveer added the vow of purity of body and mind (celibacy, BRAHMACHARYA). He established the four-fold order (CHATURVIDH SANGHA) consisting of monks (SADHUS), nuns (SADHVIS), laymen (SHRAAVAKs) and laywomen (SHRAAVIKAs).

Bhagwaan Mahaveer emphasized that all events in the universe including those in the life of man take place according to the laws of nature. There is no interference of any superhuman or supernatural being in our lives. Thus performing any ritual to please God or demigods is futile. It is the purity of our feelings and thoughts that leads to spiritual progress. He renounced all rituals including those involving sacrifices of materials and animals. By scrupulously practicing the five vows, he showed the path to spiritual progress. He spent the last thirty years of his life in such spiritual pursuit.

At the age of seventy-two, in 527 B.C., Bhagwaan Mahaveer left the human body and attained salvation (NIRVANA) at Pavapuri in the state of Bihar in India. Since then Pavapuri has become a place of pilgrimage for Jains. Soon after Bhagwaan Mahaveer's NIRVANA, Gautam Swami attained omniscience.

We Jains celebrate Bhagwaan Mahaveer's NIRVANA and Gautam Swami's attainment of omniscience during the Festival of Lights (DIWALI).

* * * * * * *

"A large amount of literature, both ancient and modern, is available on the life and activities of Mahavira; and many myths, miracles and legends have grown about his personality, as usual with all religious dignitaries. Scientific and historical scrutiny unaffected by sectarian prejudice and religious bias is made difficult by the very nature of the sources from which the information has to be gleaned. What I have attempted (written) above is a bare outline of Mahavira's biography. If it is difficult, or beyond the means of historical study, to know all about Mahavira, in my humble opinion, it is more important to understand and put into practice the principles preached by Mahavira than to discuss this detail or that about his personal life." - Dr. A. N. Upadhye, the well-known Jain scholar of modern times

* * * * * * *

Mother's Dreams

by Duli Chandra Jain

All mothers have dreams. Bhagwaan Mahaveer's mother, Queen Trishala, also had dreams. A few months before Mahaveer's birth, Queen Trishala saw a number of dreams, fourteen according some scriptures. When she woke up, she told her husband, King Siddhaarth, about the dreams. King Siddhaarth asked the scholars of his court who explained the meaning of Queen Trishala's dreams. The king and queen were very happy to learn that a supreme personage would be born who would attain absolute knowledge (KEVAL JNAAN) and would show the path to real happiness.

Mother Trishala's dreams and their symbolic meanings are as follows:

1. **A magnificent large elephant having four beautiful tusks:** Queen Trishala would give birth to a child with exceptionally good character. The four tusks signify the four components of the Jain religious order consisting of monks, nuns, laymen and laywomen.

2. **A beautiful, tame, white bullock:** The child would be highly religious. He would cultivate religion.

3. **A handsome, playful lion:** The child would be brave and powerful. He would control his sensual desires as a lion controls other animals. He would be a protector of the world which is like a jungle.

4. **Lakshmi_the goddess of prosperity being anointed with water:** Mahaveer would enjoy wealth and splendor. He would be a TEERTHANKAR, the supreme benefactor of all.

5. **A beautiful garland descending from the sky:** Mahaveer would be respected by all.

6. **The Moon:** The child would alleviate the sufferings of all living beings. He would bring peace to the world. The Moon makes a certain flower bloom. Similarly, Mahaveer would help in the spiritual progress of humanity at large.

7. **The Sun:** Mahaveer would have supreme knowledge (brilliance) and would dispel the darkness of delusion from the masses.

8. **A flag:** Bhagwaan Mahaveer would carry the banner of religion. He would reinstate the religious order.

9. **A golden vase filled with pure water:** Mahaveer would be full of compassion for all living beings. He would be the supreme religious personality like the ornament (KALASH) on the steeple of a temple.

10. **A lotus lake:** A lotus remains above water although its roots are in mud. Similarly, even while living the life of a householder, Mahaveer would be beyond worldly attachment. The masses would gather around him. Lotus-shaped assemblies (SAMAVASHARAN) would be organized where Mahaveer would preach the principles of religion.

11. **The ocean:** Mahaveer would have a serene, placid and pleasant disposition. He would achieve infinite perception and knowledge.

12. **A celestial abode:** Mahaveer would be honored by heavenly beings.

13. **A heap of jewels:** Mahaveer would have innumerable virtues. He would attain supreme spiritualism.

14. **A smokeless flame:** Gold is purified with fire. Similarly, Mahaveer would reform and reinstate the religious order. He would remove blind faith and orthodox rituals. Further, he would burn (destroy) his karma and attain salvation.

Some scriptures describe sixteen dreams of Mother Trishala. They include **a pair of fish** and **a lofty throne**. The pair of fish signifies that the child would be extremely handsome. The throne is symbolic of high spiritual status.

Mothers of all TEERTHANKARs have had similar dreams. During many religious celebrations, we Jains perform the dream ceremony to remind us of the fact that all mothers (and fathers too) have dreams about their sons and daughters. During such celebrations we should make a determination to fulfill our parents' dreams. We should lead a good clean life and should make a sincere effort to improve life on earth for all living beings. Our lives should be the true celebrations of mother's dreams.

Bibliography:

'TEERTHANKAR MAHAVEER AUR UNKI ACHARYA PARAMPARA' by Dr. Nemi Chandra Shastri, Jyotishaacharya

* * * * * * *

Sacred is the doorstep of the temple at which a gold ring offered by a king and penny offered by a pauper have the same value.　　　　A Hindi Poet

* * * * * * *

The Story Of Mahaveer And Chandkaushik

Retold by Duli Chandra Jain

(The writer has presented his own view of the story.)

This is a story about Bhagwaan Mahaveer when he was a monk. He meditated and performed penance including fasting. He was in the pursuit of truth. He traveled from place to place, from one village to another.

Once Mahaveer was going to the village of Vaachala. On the way there lived a deadly snake called Chandkaushik, a poisonous cobra. People in the surrounding area lived in terror of Chandkaushik. It was said that Chandkaushik could kill just by casting his glance upon a person or animal.

When people learned that Mahaveer intended to follow the route where Chandkaushik lived, they requested him to take another path to Vaachala. However, Mahaveer had no fear because he practiced supreme nonviolence. He had no hatred towards anyone or anything. He considered fear and hatred as violence of self. As a nonviolent and truthful individual he had nothing to be afraid of. He was at peace with himself and with all living beings of the universe. The absence of fear and hatred produced a glow of serenity and compassion on Bhagwaan Mahaveer's face. He took the dangerous path where Chandkaushik lived.

On the way, Mahaveer stopped to meditate. His eyes were closed. As he was pondering over the true nature of the universe, he had the following thoughts: 'The survival of the world depends on the harmony between man and nature. Each living being has a unique place in the scheme of things.' Feelings of peace, tranquility and concern for the welfare of all living beings were reflected on his face. The milk of kindness and concern for the well-being of all living beings was flowing from Mahaveer's heart.

When Chandkaushik came out of his abode, he saw Bhagwaan Mahaveer. Chandkaushik did not feel threatened. He saw no reason to be afraid of Mahaveer. The dangerous cobra felt humbled by the power of good feelings which Bhagwaan Mahaveer had for all living beings.

When Bhagwaan Mahaveer opened his eyes, he saw Chandkaushik but he had no feelings of attachment (RAAG) or aversion (DWESH). He continued on his way to Vaachala.

The moral of the story is that if we are afraid of someone, if we have hatred towards an individual, if we consider a person to be inferior to us, if we suspect someone, or if we have thoughts of revenge, it shows on our face. This kind of behavior constitutes violence and it may lead to further violence, mental as well as physical. We should avoid such mental violence. Peace and harmony in society comes from feelings of love and equality of all human beings.

Our practice of nonviolence begins with vegetarianism. Next comes minimizing violence in our daily activities. We should not hurt others' feelings by indulging in suspicion, intrigue, hatred, prejudice or notions of superiority. Our behavior should lead to trust, understanding and friendship. This is Bhagwaan Mahaveer's concept of nonviolence.

* * * * * * *

An individual does not become a SHRAMAN (one who believes in self-help for spiritual progress) by pulling out his hair; a person does not become a BRAHMIN (a scholar) by chanting 'OM' (a sacred word which represents the five benevolent personalities, ARIHANT, SIDDHA, ACHARYA, UPAADHYAAYA and SADHU); one does not become a MUNI (monk) by living in a forest; and, one does not become a TAPASVI (he who performs penance) by wearing garments made of grass or bark (that is, rough garments).

UTTARAADHYAYAN SUTRA

* * * * * * *

⑨

What Are You?
by Devendra Kumar Jain

Friends, see yourself, with the right view,
In this great wide world, what are you?
Are you the hand, the eye, the ear?
With what you touch and see and hear.

Think, when you say: 'This is my hand',
It shows an owner quite different,
From heart, from body and from mind,
Who is that owner? Think and find.

Neither body nor mind, that owner is soul;
Just goods and things are not life's goal.

*   *   *   *   *   *   *

When religion goes to people's heads,
Steel is sharpened,
Tongues grow cruel,
Poisoned by black snakes of hatred,
Red blood in the veins
Turns dark,
Lips beautiful to kiss
Foam.

Amrita Pritam
Well-known Indian poetess
*   *   *   *   *   *   *

10 A Story From The Life Of Bhagwaan Parshvanath
by Nidhi Dugar

In India, the city of Varanasi, commonly known as Banaras, is a very beautiful city, with its magnificent temples and majestic buildings, on the banks of the holy river Ganges. It has been the center of learning and religion from ancient times. About 250 years before Bhagwaan Mahaveer's time, there ruled the eminent Jain King Ashva Sen with his beautiful wife, Queen Vama Devi. Their extraordinary son, above and beyond all others, was Prince Parshva Kumar.

One day, when Parshva Kumar was sitting in his majestic palace, he heard a commotion in the street below. When he looked out of the window, he saw an enormous parade. People were carrying delicious sweets, beautiful garments and precious jewelry. He asked his mother what the parade was about. Queen Vama Devi replied that the hermit Kamath, who was renowned for his five-fire penance (PANCHAAGNI TAPAH), had arrived in the city of Varanasi. Therefore, people were going to his hermitage (ASHRAM) to pay their respect. The queen also wished to go and greet Kamath. She asked Parshva Kumar to accompany her.

Parshva Kumar had heard of the hermit and had mixed feelings about him. He knew something was not right about Kamath and his penance. Nevertheless Parshva Kumar respected his mother's feelings and he readily agreed to accompany her.

When they arrived at the hermitage, they saw Kamath performing the difficult penance of five fires. It was quite an impressive show. Huge logs of wood were on all four sides of Kamath and hot summer sun was shining from above. The hermit was seemingly meditating about God, soul and worldly delusions (MAYA). People were bowing to him with deep respect.

On seeing the hermit in meditation, Parshva Kumar had many thoughts. Through his intellect and experience, he realized that Kamath's penance was of no avail. He said to himself, "What kind of meditation is this? This is wrong, meaningless. Many living beings including humans are suffering in the heat. There are creatures living in the logs of wood. Many lives are being lost in the fire. It appears that this entire show has been put on to charm the people. This indiscriminate ritual of punishing the body is neither a religious practice nor a spiritual experience. A religious practice or spiritual experience should have a rationale. It should be initiated after a careful study." For a moment, Parshva Kumar was in a dilemma. On one hand, he did not want to hurt the feelings of Kamath and of his followers who deeply respected him. On the other hand, he strongly felt that it was his duty to show the right from wrong.

Finally, Parshva Kumar stepped forward and said to Kamath, "O respected hermit, do you realize that by burning the logs of wood, you are inadvertently destroying the dwellings of many creatures? Do you know that living beings are being killed in the fire? What good is this type of meditation? How can this give you or anyone a spiritual experience?"

The hermit became very angry. He was burning with rage. He replied, "Parshva, you are a KSHATRIYA (one who belongs to the ruling class) prince. You are not a Brahmin who is a scholar and a priest. How can you know what is meditation? A prince should not interfere in religious matters. A prince should look after his kingdom. He should play games and sports. So go and enjoy yourself."

Parshva Kumar stayed calm. However, he wanted to prove his point. He wanted to show that creatures were burning in the logs. A wood cutter was called and the prince ordered him to chop the logs as carefully as possible.

Inside one of the logs, there was a pair of half-burned snakes. People in the crowd saw them. The hermit was bewildered. He had no words to express himself. He felt ashamed and fallen from grace. Parshva Kumar noticed that the snakes were near death. Parshva Kumar recited the NAMOKAAR mantra. Everybody was genuinely concerned for the well-being of the snakes. Feelings of compassion filled the air. The snakes died peacefully. This resulted in their being reborn as heavenly beings (DEV and DEVI). Thus Parshva Kumar helped change the future lives of the snakes. Understanding NAMOKAAR mantra can lead to the knowledge of the principles of religion. It can improve our lives.

Parshva Kumar showed the meaning of true

religion by practicing it himself. He set the example of a moral and virtuous life. Parshva Kumar ultimately became Parshvanath, the twenty-third TEERTHANKAR of the Jains. Most modern historians believe that he was one of the earliest historical personalities.

The moral of the story is that we should always carefully think and plan before performing any religious activity and make sure that it does not become a ritual.

* * * * * * *

The monk (or any individual), who indulges in telling the fortune of men and women by looking at the lines in their palms, who interprets the dreams and thus tries to foretell the future events (in the life of an individual), who indulges in charming the masses by miracles, who gets involved in describing and performing occult, superstitious rites for obtaining a male (or female) child, and whose livelihood is based on the practices [of MANTRA and TANTRA (occult rites)] involving mysticism, will not have any refuge at the time of the fruition of karma.

UTTARAADHYAYAN SUTRA

* * * * * * *

⑪ Concept Of Universe In Jainism

Universe means the things around us. Whatever we see is part of the universe. There are many things in the universe that we can not see such as air, space and time. Thus universe contains things that we can see and things that we can not see. In other words, the universe means the totality of all things that exist.

We want to acquire knowledge of all things and events in the universe. We want to know the basic substances or entities (DRAVYAS) the universe is made of. Did anybody create the universe? How do the various events in the universe take place? Does anybody run or manage the universe? Answers to such questions make up our concept of the universe.

We know that there are material objects in the universe. The sun, the earth, the moon and the stars are there. There are people, cows, birds and trees. There is energy in its many forms, heat, light, sound and electricity. There is the space in which the objects of the universe are situated. There is the time. There are living beings in the universe and there are non-living objects. Living beings grow. They have various life processes such as respiration, secretion of chemical substances called enzymes and excretion of waste material.

We see that changes take place in various objects. We put a seed in the ground and a plant grows. In autumn, the leaves of the trees change color and fall. It snows and its rains. Wind blows and fire burns.

The question arises: How do these changes take place? The Jain religion gives a very logical answer to this. According to Jainism, all objects of the universe change according to their own basic properties. The substances of the universe interact with each other. These interactions lead to the various changes and events in the universe. The sun shines on the waters of lakes, rivers and oceans. The water is turned into vapor which rises to form clouds. Depending upon the atmospheric conditions, the clouds produce rain or snow. Thus, according to Jainism, nature and the laws of nature are responsible for all that happens in the universe. There is no supernatural entity running the universe.

Jainism also believes that the basic substances of the universe can not be created out of nothing. All basic substances of the universe have always existed. They do undergo changes on account of interactions between themselves. All changes take place because of the properties of the substances involved. The universe has no beginning and no end. Nobody created the universe, nobody protects it and nobody will bring it to an end.

There are six entities in the universe. They are of two kinds: Living (JEEV) and non-living (AJEEV).

The living entity is soul (ATMA). Soul has consciousness (awareness of things and events, CHETANA), perception (DARSHAN) and knowledge

(JNAAN). The perception and knowledge of worldly souls are partly covered (to varying degrees) by karma particles.

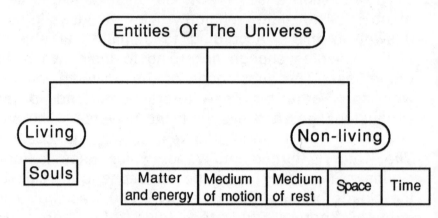

All living beings have souls. There are innumerable souls in the universe. All souls are basically identical. Each soul is independent. When a worldly soul takes up a material body, a new life begins. A living being grows and other life processes take place because of the presence of a soul in the body. When the soul leaves the body, the living being dies. A worldly soul interacts with other living beings and with other entities of the universe because it has a material body. SIDDHAs are pure souls that have no material attachment. Thus they do not interfere in the events of the universe.

The remaining five entities of the universe are non-living. They are: Matter and energy (PUDGALs), medium of motion (DHARM), medium of rest (ADHARM), space (AAKAASH) and time (KAAL).

Each entity of the universe is distinct. Matter

can not be changed into space and space can not be changed into time. A soul can not be changed into matter or space. Further, a soul can not be created out of matter, energy, space and/or time. No entity of the universe can be totally destroyed. Modern science deals with matter, energy, space and time. According to the Jain belief, soul can not be detected by material devices or instruments. It can not be detected by our senses either. We can not see it or touch it.

Jainism considers matter and energy as one and the same basic entity. Thus according to Jainism, matter can be converted into energy and energy can be converted into matter. Such conversions occur in nature, and in scientific experiments. Einstein's theory of relativity showed that

$E = mc^2$.

[Energy = (mass)x(velocity of light)^2].

Matter and energy (material objects) can be detected by means of our senses and by using scientific instruments. No other entity of the universe can be detected by means of our senses or by using any material devices.

The next two non-living entities, the medium of motion and the medium of rest, support the state of motion and the state of rest of living beings and material bodies.

The fourth non-living entity, space, accommodates all other entities of the universe. Space is divided into two parts: the physical space (LOKAAKAASH) where all living and non-living entities are found, and, the empty space

(ALOKAAKAASH) which is infinite and lies beyond the physical space.

The last non-living entity is time. It fills the entire physical space. Time has no beginning and no end. It is responsible for ideas about past, present and future. It helps in the growth and development of living entities. Time helps bring about the changes that take place in the universe.

* * * * * * *

UVASANT KHEEN MOHO MAGGAM JIN BHASIDEN SAMUVAGADO

NAANAANU MAGGA CHAARI NIVVAAN PURAM VAJADI DHEERO

Suppressing or annihilating the veil of ignorance which clouds the faculties of perception and will, well-equipped with the three jewels which constitute the path revealed by JIN, the undaunted pilgrim that conquered the suffering and pain due to the environment, beckoned by the ideal of self-knowledge, the soul wades through the path and reaches the divine place of perfection.

Acharya Kundkund in Panchaastikaayasaar

* * * * * * *

(12) What Does An Elephant Look Like?

An elephant once came to a small town. People had read and heard of elephants but no one in the town had ever seen an elephant. So a huge crowd gathered around the elephant. It was an occasion for great fun, especially for children.

Five blind men also lived in that town. They had never seen an elephant. When they heard that an elephant was in town, they were eager to find out what an elephant looked like. They could not see and so they were somewhat disappointed. Then somebody suggested that they could touch and feel the elephant. Thus they could get some idea of what an elephant looked like.

The five blind men went to the town square where the elephant was. People stepped aside so that they could go near the elephant and touch him. They were happy to have touched the elephant.

Later, they sat down and started discussing their impressions. One blind man, who had touched the trunk of the elephant, said that the elephant was like a thick branch of a tree. The second blind man who had touched the tail of the elephant, said that the elephant was like a snake or rope. The third blind man had felt a leg of the elephant. He said that the shape of an elephant was like a pillar. The fourth blind man had touched an ear of the elephant. He said that the elephant was like a huge fan. The fifth blind man who had touched the side of the elephant, said that the elephant was like a wall.

They discussed and argued. Each one was quite sure that his image was correct. Obviously, they could not agree regarding the form of an elephant. Finally, they decided to go to a wise man in the village who had seen the elephant with his own eyes.

The wise man said, "Gentlemen, all five of you are right. However, each one of you has touched only one part of the body of the elephant. Thus you have only a partial 'view' of the elephant. If you put together your partial 'views' in proper order, you will get an idea of what an elephant looks like."

The moral of the story is that each one of us sees things from our own point of view. Consequently, we obtain a view that is only partially correct. Hence we should also try to understand others' viewpoints. This will enable us to get a proper and complete perspective on events and situations. The differences between individuals, societies, religions and nations can be resolved if people try to accommodate others' views.

Religion, truth and reality are like an elephant. We have to look at them from a variety of angles of vision. Jainism calls this relativism (SYAADAVAAD) or the doctrine of multiplicity of viewpoints (ANEKAANTAVAAD). Other religions like Hinduism and Buddhism have similar theories.

Song Of Soul

by Sahajanand Varni

(Translated into English by Shri Mahesh Chandra, M.A., LL.B.)

Pristine, eternal, wishless, free
Knower, seer, such soul is me!

I am what Supreme Being is;
What myself is, the same God is;
With this sole external difference,
Here passions, there indifference.

My real self like SIDDHA is;
Infinite power, knowledge, bliss;
Losing knowledge and contentment,
I am left beggar, ignorant.

None else bestows pain and pleasure;
Love and anger are grief's treasure;
Self from non-self, I distinguish;
And there will be no anguish.

Whose names are Brahma, Hari, Buddha,
Ishwar, Jin, Vishnu and Shiva;
Leaving passions, I reach that goal;
No distress then will be for soul.

This world does function by itself;
I may not indulge in non-self;
May alien influence get away.
In bliss, for ever, may I sway.

Living Beings
(Souls)

Soul is living entity. Acharya Umaswati has written that the distinguishing characteristic of a soul is consciousness.[1] Jains believe that the difference between a worldly living being and a non-living object is that a living being has a soul while the non-living object does not have soul. The soul fills the entire body of a living being. The life processes of a living body take place because of the presence of the soul. When the soul leaves the body, the living being dies. The soul then assumes another body. The soul takes the shape of the body of the living being and grows as the body develops. This is the concept of reincarnation in Jainism. It is the process of interaction between a worldly soul and other entities of the universe.

Classification of living beings

The living beings (JEEVs — worldly souls having bodies) are classified into two categories: Mobile (TRAS) and immobile (STHAAVAR).

The immobile living beings have only one sense, the sense of touch (SPARSH). They are of five kinds:

1. Earth-bodied (PRITHVI KAAYIK)
2. Water-bodied (JAL KAAYIK)
3. Fire-bodied (AGNI KAAYIK)
4. Air-bodied (VAAYU KAAYIK)

---

[1] UPAYOGO LAKSHNAM - Tattvaarth Sutra, Chapter 2, aphorism 8.

5. Vegetable-bodied (VANASPATI KAAYIK)

The famous Indian scientist, Sir Jagadish Chandra Bose, was the first to demonstrate that plants respond to various kinds of stimuli. Thus he showed that plants have life and the sense of touch. Plants have plasmodesmata which are delicate strands connecting the living protoplasm of neighboring cells. These enable the correlation of the functions of the cells. These may also be responsible for the transmission of stimuli through the tissue. This may be considered the sense of touch in plants.

The mobile living beings have two or more senses. Their classification is:

Two-sensed (DWEENDRIYA) with senses of touch and taste

Three-sensed (TRINDRIYA) with senses of touch, taste and smell

Four-sensed (CHATURINDRIYA) with senses of touch, taste, smell and sight

Five-sensed (PANCHENDRIYA) with senses of touch, taste, smell, sight and hearing.

Higher forms of life, man and animals, have all five senses. They also have faculty of thinking (MANAH).

Classification of souls

Souls are classified into two categories: the liberated (MUKTA) souls and worldly (SAMSAARI) souls. The worldly souls are associated with matter of various kinds. On account of this association, they interact with other entities of the universe. The real attributes of worldly souls are obscured by eight kinds of karma particles. They are:

1. Perception-obscuring karma (DARSHANAAVARNI KARMA)
2. Knowledge-obscuring karma (JNAANAAVARNI KARMA)
3. Feeling-producing karma (VEDANEEYA KARMA)
4. Deluding karma (MOHANEEYA KARMA)
5. Life-span-determining karma (AAYU KARMA)
6 Physique-determining karma (NAAM KARMA)
7. Status-determining karma (GOTRA KARMA)
8. Obstructing karma (ANTARAAYA KARMA)

The perception-obscuring, knowledge-obscuring, deluding and obstructing karmas cover the intrinsic attributes of a soul and thus they are called GHAATIYA karmas. An individual becomes omniscient (KEVALI) on shedding GHAATIYA karmas. The remaining four karmas influence the physical existence of a living being and are called AGHAATIYA karmas.

The karma particles are very fine particles of matter. They can not be detected by our senses or by any instruments. When a living being dies and takes up another life, the karma particles are carried along by the soul.

A living being can modify the karma particles in his/her possession. A person can control the influence of karma on his/her soul by having proper feelings and thoughts. This implies that the higher the form of life, the greater the control it has on the karmas. In this respect, human life is the highest form of life.

When a soul sheds all karma particles, it

becomes liberated. This is the process of attaining NIRVANA. The liberated souls have the following eight attributes. Indeed, these are the attributes of a pure soul.

Attribute	Acquired by destroying
Absolute rationalism (KSHAAYIK SAMYAKTVA)	Deluding karma
Absolute infinite perception (ANANT DARSHAN)	Perception-obscuring karma
Absolute infinite knowledge (ANANT JNAAN)	Knowledge-obscuring karma
Equality of status (AGURULAGHUTVA)	Status-determining karma
Eternity (AVAGAAHANATVA)	Life-span-determining karma
Subtlety (SOOKSHMATVA)	Physique-determining karma
Non-interference (AVYAABAADHATVA)	Feeling-producing karma
Infinite bliss (ANANT VEERYA)	Obstructing karma

We are worldly souls. We hope to make spiritual progress and eventually free ourselves from the bondage of karma.

Jain Theory Of Karma
by Duli Chandra Jain

Rashmi: Ma, we know that there are six entities in the universe. These are souls, matter, medium of motion, medium of rest, space and time. We also learned that the universe has no beginning and no end. Further, the universe has neither been created by anyone nor is it being run by any supernatural personality. Now the question arises: How does the universe function?

Ma: The universe functions because of the interactions of its various entities. The interactions take place according to the basic qualities of the six entities.

Rashmi: What about living beings? Who or what determines the course of their lives?

Ma: That is an important question. Worldly living beings are souls with material bodies. Thus we are sort of a combinations of two entities; soul and matter. Obviously, we (all living beings) have the attributes of a pure soul. These attributes are, however, obscured because of our association with matter. We interact with matter and with other beings of the universe. Such interactions determine the course of our lives.

Ranjana: Can you please explain these interactions?

Ma: We build a fire, cook our food, make or buy clothes, read books, talk with each other, arrange our rooms. All these activities involve interactions between matter and living beings. In these activities, we think, we feel pleasure or pain, we become happy or unhappy, we get angry or proud. We have a variety of feelings and emotions. These are also the results of our interactions with our surroundings.

Ranita: How do these interactions influence our lives and our future?

Ma: These feelings and emotions result in the influx and bondage of karmas which may influence our lives.

Ranita: Ma, what are karmas?

Ma: Karmas are very fine particles of matter which are associated with worldly souls.

Rashmi: What do karmas do to a living being?

Ma: Rashmi, in general, karmas affect the lives of worldly souls. Feelings of happiness and misery are caused by karmas. A worldly soul suffers through cycles of birth and rebirth because of the association of karmas.

Ranjana: Ma, does anything else affect our lives?

Ma: Yes, in addition to karmas, there are pseudokarmas (NOKARMAS) which have some effect on our lives. Our parents, relatives, friends, teachers, books, food, medicine and other things are pseudokarmas.

Ranjana: Many good pseudokarmas are given to us by our parents. Does God give us good karmas and pseudokarmas?

Ma: It is true that some pseudokarmas are provided by others. However, we ourselves are responsible for most of our pseudokarmas and for all our karmas. According to Jainism, God does not reward or punish us.

Rashmi: How do we obtain karmas?

Ma: Our actions, feelings and emotions cause the influx and binding of karmas. Good deeds and feelings bring good karmas while feelings of violence, anger and greed lead to the influx of bad karmas.

Ranita: Ma, what is meant by influx and bondage of karmas?

Ma: When a worldly living being indulges in good and bad deeds and thoughts, karma particles come towards his soul. This is known as influx (AASHRAV) of karma. On account of the passions, the karma particles get associated with the soul. This is called bondage (BANDH) of karma.

Rashmi: Are there any features of bondage of karma?

Ma: Yes, there are four features of bondage of karma. They are:

(a) Nature of karmas: Nature means the kind of karmas that are associated with the soul. Karmas are of eight kinds:

1. Perception-obscuring (DARSHANAAVARNI) karma
2. Knowledge-obscuring (JNAANAAVARNI) karma
3. Feeling-producing (VEDANEEYA) karma
4. Deluding (MOHANEEYA) karma
5. Life-span-determining (AAYU) karma

6 Physique-determining (NAAM) karma

7. Status-determining (GOTRA) karma

8. Obstructing (ANTARAAYA) karma

(b)Quantity of karma particles: The number of karma particles which are bound to the soul.

(c)Duration of karma particles: Duration means the time during which the karmas will remain attached to the soul.

(d)Intensity of fruition: This means the severity of the consequences of the karmas.

Ranita: Ma, what is fruition of karma?

Ma: When we have feelings of pleasure or pain because of karma particles attached to our souls, it is called fruition of karma.

Ranjana: What determines the nature, extent, duration and intensity of fruition of karma?

Ma: The nature (kind) and quantity of karmas are determined by YOGA—the combined activity of body, speech and mind. The nature of the activity determine the kind of karma while the extent of activity determines the quantity of karma particles. The duration and intensity of fruition are determined by the intensity of passions of the individual.

Rashmi: Ma, according to Jainism, God does not help us. Does it mean that our lives are wholly dependent on karmas?

Ma: Rashmi, we do not have to be wholly dependent on karmas. True, God does not help us but we can help ourselves. By keeping good attitude towards life and by having pure thoughts and feelings, even when things go against our wishes, we can lessen the impact of karmas and pseudokarmas on our lives.

Rashmi: Are wealth, poverty, material comforts and sickness results of good and bad karmas?

Ma: These may or may not be the consequences of our past karmas. These are material things and as such they can only affect our bodies. They can not affect our souls. The feelings of happiness and misery which we have are the results of our past or present karmas.

Rashmi: Can you please explain this in some detail?

Ma: Let us take the example of sickness. Our health may be the consequence of our past karma or of poor diet or lack of proper rest. We may cry over spilled milk, feel miserable because of sickness and let the karmas and pseudokarmas produce an undesirable effect on our lives. Alternatively, we may consider that the soul and body are two different entities. The disease can only affect our bodies and not our souls. We may keep our cool, take proper rest and medicine, and make a determination to be more careful in the future. In this manner, we can avoid or minimize the negative effect of karmas and pseudokarmas on our lives.

The above example shows that effort does make the difference. According to the Jain theory of karma, nothing is predestined. However, it is the higher forms of life that have more control over what happens to them. Man is the highest form of life in this respect.

Ranita: What is so special about the Jain theory of karma?

Ma: Karma theory says that there is no interference of any superhuman power in our lives. All souls are independent and equal. Only we can help ourselves. The same laws of nature apply to all living beings and to other entities of the universe. The same rules apply to all regardless of their religious beliefs, color or creed.

Ranjana: Ma, if God does not help us then why do we pray to ARIHANTs, SIDDHAs, Bhagwaan Mahaveer and other TEERTHANKARs?

Ma: When we pray to VEETARAAG JIN, we are reminded of the attributes of the pure soul. We remember the good deeds of Bhagwaan Mahaveer and other TEERTHANKARs. We are reminded of the teachings of our religion. Thus we learn to have good thoughts and feelings. We make a determination to do good deeds in our lives. We learn to have peace of mind. These lessen the negative influence of bad karma on our lives.

My Aspirations

Pandit Jugal Kishore Mukhtar's **MERI BHAAVANA**[*]

He who conquered love and hatred,
And vanquished sensual temptation,
True cosmic knowledge who attained
And showed the path to salvation;

> Some may call Him Buddha, Hari, Jin,
> Or may call Him Brahma, Supreme;
> His thoughts and deep devotion may
> Be in my heart and mind and dream.

Who do not long for sensual zest,
Whose feelings are gentle and right;
In well-being of world and self,
Who do endeavor day and night;

> Who do penance of selflessness
> And who have no regrets in life;
> To lessen suffering of this world;
> Such learned sages do strife.

May I always look up to them
And may I keep them in my mind;
Practice their conduct in my life,
I wish my mind be so inclined.

---

[*] English Adaptation by Devendra Kumar Jain. Reprinted from "Essentials of Jainism", published by Jain Center of Greater Boston.

May I never injure a life;
Of lying, may I never think;
Not wanting others' wealth and spouse,
Contentment nectar may I drink.

May egotism I never feel;
Angry, may never I become;
On seeing others' worldly wealth,
To envy may I not succumb.

May I always feel and ponder
To act in true and sincere way;
I always may do good to all,
As far as I can, everyday.

For living beings of the world,
Feelings of friendship may I show;
For woeful creatures, from my heart,
May stream of kindness ever flow.

The cruel, wicked and evildoers,
My mood and mind may not resent;
May thoughts of mine be so mended,
Of others I may be tolerant.

My heart may be so full of love,
Whenever I see a noble man;
My mind may be so full of joy;
I serve him as much as I can.

May I never be ungrateful;
Malice never be in my mind;
May I not see faults of people;
High virtues may I always find.

Let someone call me good or bad,
Let riches come or turn away,
Whether I live for million years,
Or I face death this very day,

      Whether someone does frighten me,
      Or even tempt me in some way.
      May my steps never falter
      From proven good and righteous way.

Neither may I be too joyous,
Nor may I be nervous in pain;
I may not dread stormy river,
A jungle, ghost or rough mountain.

      Firm, unshaken and well-balanced,
      My mind may ever grow and grow;
      In beloved's passing, evil's face,
      Endurance may I ever show.

May worldly creatures be blissful,
Uneasiness may no one feel;
Forgetting ill will, pride and guilt,
New songs of joy may sing with zeal.

      May truth be talk of every home,
      There be no sign of evil act;
      Enlightened people may improve,
      Fruits of this life may get, in fact.

Misfortune, dread may never come;
Bountiful rains come well in time;
May rulers always be righteous,
May justice be even, sublime.

Disease and famine may not be;
May people have plenty and peace;
Nonviolence be the rule of world,
May world be full of joy and ease.

May mutual love pervade the world,
And dark delusions fade away;
Untrue, unkind, intriguing, harsh,
Such words, no one may ever say.

May all become YUGVEER* at heart;
Welfare and peace may all attain;
Facing all sorrows with patience,
Nature of truth may all men gain.

----

* This is the pen name of Pandit Jugal Kishore Mukhtar.
It means 'hero of the age'.

* * * * * * *

MAITRI PRAMOD KAARUNYA MAADHYASTHAANI CHA
SATTVA GUNAADHIK KLISHYAMAAN AVINAYESHU.

Benevolence towards all living beings, joy at the sight
of the virtuous, compassion and sympathy for the afflicted,
and, tolerance towards the insolent and ill-behaved.
He who conducts himself in this manner is able to
practice nonviolence and other vows to perfection.

- Acharya Umaswati
in Tattvaarth Sutra

* * * * * * *

Two Sides Of The Shield
By Neeta Shah

The principles of Jain philosophy are based on the theory of relativism which is called SYAADAVAAD in Sanskrit. The word SYAADAVAAD is composed of two words, SYAT meaning 'in a sense' or 'from a certain point of view', and VAAD meaning 'principle' or 'school of thought'.

An object from one point of view appears to be of a certain type, while from another point of view the same object appears to be of a different nature. Relativism implies that to comprehend the full aspect of anything, one must take into account many different points of view. Because of this belief, the principle of relativism (SYAADAVAAD) is also called the principle of multiplicity of viewpoints (ANEKAANTAVAAD) — a school of thought which takes into account multiple points of view.

Here is a parable which illustrates the concept of multiplicity of viewpoints.

On the outskirts of a town, in a park, stood a statue in honor of one of its heroes. The statue had a sword in one hand and a shield in the other. One side of the shield was silver-plated while the other side was gold-plated.

The town people used to visit the park with their children. One day, a mother took her two young sons, Rajeev and Ravi, to the park. The mother sat on a bench and her sons got busy in playing hide and seek. In the course of their play, they came across the statue. Rajeev approached it from one side while Ravi, from the other side. They were very excited to see the beautiful statue and started admiring it.

The younger child, Ravi said, "What a majestic statue! And look at the shield. It seems to be made of pure silver."

Rajeev said, "What! It is gold-plated. Ravi, you are too young to know the difference between gold and silver."

Ravi was surprised to hear his brother say that he did not know the difference between gold and silver. He again looked at the shield carefully and said, "Brother, I can clearly see that the color of the shield is silver. I do not see any color of gold. The rays of the sun are shining on your side of the statue. That is why you are saying that the shield is gold-plated."

Rajeev said, "I can see that the gold color of the shield is not due to the rays of the sun. The shield is gold-plated."

Ravi said, "How can it be gold-plated? It is white as silver. Maybe it is not made of solid silver and it is just silver-plated."

Rajeev was getting upset. His little brother would not listen to him. He would not understand that the shield was gold-plated. He said to Ravi, "It seems that you have lost the sense of colors of gold and silver. Are you colorblind? I am absolutely certain that the shield is gold-plated."

Ravi's feelings were deeply hurt and so he started to cry. Their mother came running and asked them, "What is the argument about?" Rajeev explained the matter. The mother who was standing in the middle, could see both sides of the shield and so she had a smile on her face. She asked Rajeev and Ravi to exchange their places and look at the shield again. They promptly obliged. Their anger disappeared. They both could see why the other had previously insisted that he was right. Both clung to their mother.

The moral of this story is that if we try to examine a given situation from other's viewpoint as well as from our own viewpoint, our differences will have much less negative influence on our lives. The same thing can be examined from many different points of view. To properly understand it, we must take all the different aspects into consideration.

The principle of multiplicity of viewpoints can help us in resolving our differences and in minimizing the violence of feelings and thoughts. Thus multiplicity of viewpoints and relativism are integral parts of our religion

Bibliography:
"Jainism In Nut Shell" by Muni Kirti Vijay, published by Jain Gyana Mandir, Bombay.

Three Jewels Of Jainism

Three jewels (RATNATRAYA) of Jainism are: rational (proper) perception (SAMYAK DARSHAN), rational knowledge (SAMYAK JNAAN) and rational conduct (SAMYAK CHAARITRA). The Sanskrit word 'SAMYAK' means rational and proper. We Jains are expected to have rational perception, knowledge and conduct (life style).

Rational Perception (SAMYAK DARSHAN)

Acharya Umaswati has defined rational perception as belief in the aspects of reality.[1] In simple words, rational perception means having a proper attitude. It entails having no bias. It means accepting only what seems reasonable according to our observation, study and experience. We Jains accept what is logical and appeals to our common sense. We do not accept anything just because it is written in some book or is preached by some individual. We do not believe in dogma, hearsay and superstitions. We study religious books[2]. We study history, philosophy, science and other disciplines. We attend lectures delivered by scholars. We have discussion with scholars and among ourselves. In this manner, we learn the basic principles of religion.

---

[1] TATTVAARTH SHRADDHAANAM SAMYAK DARSHANAM - Tattvaarth Sutra, Chapter 1, Aphorism 2.

[2] This is called SWAADHYAAYA.

The famous Jain monk of modern times, Muni Nathmal writes:[3]

Jain religion is realistic. In realism, truth is not accepted due to faith either towards a person or towards a doctrine. Both are examined. Acharya Hemchandra has expressed this reality vividly. He writes: "Bhagwaan we are not on your side because of faith. Neither are we prejudiced against other thinkers because of aversion. We have examined the credibility and you have passed those tests. That is why we follow you."

Acharya Haribhadrasuri has expressed this truth squarely, saying,[4] "I am not in favor of Mahaveer due to faith in him, nor am I against other philosophers like Kapil due to aversion. I am of opinion that he should be followed whose ideas stand true on the scale of logic."

Muni Nathmal continues: The basis of this candid thought is realism. In the Puraanic period (middle ages), people zealously contended in giving hyperbolic descriptions of deities. It resulted in the human image of greatness being enshrouded in superhuman miracles. This situation was not in accordance with realism. Acharya Samantbhadra has steadfastly opposed this line of thinking. He has expressed his disapproval in accepting such

---

3 "The Struggle of Faith and Reason in Jain Tradition", published in TIRTHANKAR (English), Volume 1, July 1975, pages 67-72.

4 PAKSHPAATO NA MEY VEERE NA DWESHAH KAPILAADISHU:
YUKTIMAD VACHANAM YASYA TASYA GRAAHYAM PARIGRAHAH:

miracles as the barometer of greatness. He has tried to comprehend Mahaveer in the light of realism by tearing apart the mantle of miracles. He writes: "Bhagwaan! grandeurs like an assembly of gods, air vehicles, CHHATRA and CHOWRIE can be displayed by magicians also. Gods came to you, you possessed CHHATRA, CHOWRIE and other superhuman attributes. But that did not make you great. You are great because you unveiled truth!"

Acharya Hemchandra has also supported this line of thought. He has said: "Gods used to bow before you. This can be disputed by other philosophers or they can also call their deity revered by gods. But how can they dispute the realism propagated by you?"

Rational Knowledge And Rational Conduct

Acharya Umaswati states that reality is understood by means of experimentation and logical thinking.[5] Experimentation implies information and evidence obtained through the study of scriptures, observation and experience. This means rational knowledge is obtained through careful study and thinking. Evidently, rational perception is essential for obtaining rational knowledge.

Rational conduct entails adopting a proper life style that would help us minimize physical and mental violence of self and of other living beings. This involves living in harmony with our fellow

[5] PRAMAAN NAYAIR ADHIGAMAH - Tattvaarth Sutra, Chapter 1, Aphorism 5.

beings and with nature. It should be emphasized that proper conduct includes religious practices like study of scriptures (SWAADHYAAYA), prayer, worship, attending religious discourses (reading and discussion of scriptures, PRAAVACHAN). Our religious practice begins with these activities which are essential for learning and understanding the principles of the Jain religion, but rational conduct entails practicing the teachings of Jainism in our daily lives. We should minimize our passions, anger (KRODH), pride or ego (MAAN), deception or intrigue (MAYA) and greed (LOBH). We should practice nonviolence (AHIMSA), truth (SATYA), non-stealing (ACHAURYA), purity of body and mind (BRAHMACHARYA) and non-possessiveness (APARIGRAH).

Rational perception, rational knowledge and rational conduct comprise the path to salvation.[6]

----

6 SAMYAK DARSHAN JNAAN CHAARITRAANI MOKSH MARGAH - Tattvaarth Sutra, Chapter 1, Aphorism 1.

* * * * * * *

The happiness of heaven is indirect - it is beyond our experience. Thus we may be disinterested in it. The happiness of salvation (NIRVANA) is still more indirect. Hence we may have doubts about it. On the other hand, the peace and calm brought about by religion can be directly experienced right here. We are free to attain this happiness which is the fruit of freedom of spirit. We do not have to buy it with money. We achieve this happiness by taking a dip in the stream of satisfaction and balanced emotions   Acharya Umaswati

* * * * * * *

⑲ Spiritual Aspects Of Reality In Jainism

Jainism believes in reality. The Jain concept of reality deals with the interaction between souls and matter. What kind of interactions between worldly souls and matter are responsible for the cycles of birth and rebirth? How can a worldly soul break the cycle of birth and rebirth? What is the path to liberation of a worldly soul? The spiritual aspects of reality (TATTVAS) are the basic principles which help us answer such questions about worldly souls and their interactions with matter:

The Jain scriptures have described the following nine aspects of reality:[1]

1. Living beings (JEEV)
2. Non-living entities (AJEEV)
3. Influx of karma particles (AASHRAV)
4. Bondage of karma particles (BANDH)
5. Meritorious karma (PUNYA)
6. Demeritorious karma (PAAP)
7. Stoppage of influx of karma particles (SAMVAR)
8. Shedding of karma particles (NIRJARA)
9. Salvation (MOKSHA)

Acharya Umaswati and some other religious scholars have considered good and bad karma as part of influx and bondage of karma. Thus they have

[1] JEEVAAJEEV YA BANDHO YA PUNNAM PAAVAASHAVO TAHA: SAMVARO NIJJARA MOKKHO SANTEAE TAHIYA NAVA :14:
- UTTARAADHYAYAN SUTRA, Chapter 28.

58

described only seven aspects of reality.[2] It is obvious that basically the seven or nine aspects of reality are identical. They describe essentially the same kinds of interactions between a soul and matter.

Living beings and the non-living objects:

The worldly souls have bodies and particles of karma associated with them. On account of this association with matter, they have thoughts and feelings. They indulge in various kinds of activities of body, speech and mind. The combined activity of body, speech and mind is called **yoga**. The level of activities depends on the kind of species. Lower forms of life have very little activities of body, speech and mind. Higher forms of life have higher levels of activity. It is clear that yoga involves the interaction of living beings (JEEVs) of the universe with non-living (AJEEV) entities, such as matter, energy, space and time. Thus the living beings and non-living things are the first two aspects of reality.

Influx and bondage of meritorious and demeritorious karma:

The ordinary meaning of karma is the good and bad deeds done by a living being. But, in Jainism, the word karma has a unique meaning. Jains believe that karmas are extremely fine particles of matter that occupy the physical space. When an individual (or living being) has good or bad thoughts and feelings, the karma particles come towards

2 JEEV AJEEV AASHRAV BANDH SAMVAR NIRJARA MOKSHAAS TATTVAM -   - Tattvaarth Sutra, Chapter 1, Aphorism 4.

his/her soul. This is called influx (AASHRAV) of karma particles.

The karma particles acquired by an individual become attached to his/her soul. This is the process of bondage (BANDH) of karma. The karma particles acquired by a soul in this manner remain with the soul for some duration. In general, the karma particles in the possession of a soul lead to happiness or misery of a worldly soul. This is called **fruition** (bearing fruits) of karma.

There are four features of the karma particles obtained by a living being:

1. The nature (PRAKRITI) or kind of karma particles[3].
2. The quantity (PRADESHA) of karma particles.
3. The duration (STHITI) of karma particles, that is the time for which the karma particles remain attached to the soul.
4. The intensity or severity of fruition (ANUBHAAG) of karma particles.

The kind of karma particles and their quantity is determined by the nature and intensity of yoga. Thoughts involving violence, revenge, untruth and other undesirable feelings lead to the influx of bad karma (PAAP). Thoughts involving compassion, friendship, desire to help others and similar other feelings bring good karma (PUNYA) towards the soul.

---

[3] Such as feeling-producing karma (VEDANEEYA KARMA), perception-obscuring karma (DARSHANAAVARNI KARMA), knowledge-obscuring karma (JNAANAAVARNI KARMA), deluding karma (MOHANEEYA KARMA).

The duration of bondage of karma particles and the intensity of fruition are determined by the passions of the individual. The greater the intensity of passions (anger, ego, deceit and greed), the longer the duration of karma and the more severe the consequences of the karma. The fruition of karma gives rise to good and bad feelings and thoughts in an individual. These thoughts and feelings result in further influx and bondage of karma.

This process of interaction between a soul and karma particles is one of action and reaction. However, we may not react to the fruition of karma. We may not have undesirable thoughts and feelings as a result of fruition of karma particles. In this manner, we can control the effect of karma on our lives.

Stoppage of influx and shedding of karma:

The influx and bondage of karma particles can be compared to the inflow of water into a leaky boat. The stoppage of influx of karma is like plugging the hole in the boat. An individual can minimize his/her thought-activity (yoga) and thus reduce or stop the influx of karma. This is called SAMVAR. Stoppage of influx of karma is caused by self-restraint, conscientiousness, virtue, contemplation, endurance of suffering and proper conduct.[4] An individual can gradually relieve his/her soul of karma through penance (TAPAH) and meditation (DHYAAN). This process is called shedding of karma (NIRJARA).

---

[4] SA GUPTI SAMITI DHARM ANUPREKSHA PAREESHAHAJAYA CHAARITRAI -   - Tattvaarth Sutra, Chapter 9, Aphorism 2.

Salvation of a soul:

The stoppage of influx of karma and shedding of all karma particles in the possession of an individual's soul lead to salvation (MOKSHA).

A soul can not be detected by any physical means. Though karmas are particles of matter, they are extremely fine and so they also can not be detected by any physical means. Nevertheless, the theory of karma is a logical extension of our observations and experiences with the physical world. We see interactions between the various material objects. We see the transformations occurring due to interplay of matter of energy. The theory of karma and the aspects of reality (TATTVAS) are based on the concept of action and reaction between souls and matter.

Understanding the spiritual aspects of reality is the first step towards the liberation of soul. Our code of ethics and religious practices are based on the Jain concept of reality.

*   *   *   *   *   *   *

Jain ethics is a direct consequence of the Jain philosophy of soul and karma.

Jainism, in a way, may be regarded as a bold and daring forerunner of modern theories of utilitarianism, which, in comparison, strike as but pale and feeble attempts at evolution of only a limited variety of humanitarianism.

- Prof. Shri Krishna Saksena
in 'The Jain Religion'

*   *   *   *   *   *   *

⑳ Some Jain Religious Practices

In Jainism, religious practices include the following:

1. Temple visits
2. Religious celebrations such as celebration of Bhagwaan Mahaveer's birth, celebration of Bhagwaan Mahaveer's salvation, celebration of spiritual awareness.
3. Pilgrimages.

The above religious practices are meant to teach us the basic principles of Jainism. They inspire us to make spiritual progress. The religious practices are means and not ends in themselves. Our ultimate goal is living our daily lives according to the teachings of the Jain religion.

One may ask that if the true practice of Jainism lies in living our daily lives in accordance with its principles, then why go to temples, why pray and worship, why celebrate religious festivals, and, why go on pilgrimages? The answer lies in the two-fold purpose of Jain activities:

(a) Our religious practices remind us of the nature of reality, of our place in the universe, and, of our ultimate goal of shedding all karma and attaining absolute freedom from material bondage (Nirvana).

(b) According to Jainism, we obtain new karma particles on account of the combined activities of body, speech and mind (YOGA) and the passions (KASHAAYAs) of anger, pride, deceit and greed. We have pure thoughts, free from anger, ego and greed during our religious practices. We have peace and harmony, feelings of brotherhood and of equality of all men during religious celebrations. These good thoughts and feelings constitute righteous meditation (DHARM DHYAAN) which minimizes the negative influence of karma on our lives and brings good karma (PUNYA). When we visit temples and places of pilgrimages, we are happy and relaxed. We have peace of mind.

We should understand that there is a very fine line between a Jain religious practice and a ritual. A Jain religious activity is meant to eliminate ego and desire. If a religious activity is performed in pursuit of material gain or to seek absolution from 'sin' or with a desire to escape from misery, it becomes a ritual. Obviously, there is no place for any rituals in Jainism.

Jain Religious Celebrations

Jains celebrate numerous occasions such as the birth and salvation of TEERTHANKARs, PARYUSHAN (spiritual awareness) and JNAAN PANCHAMI (day of worship of scriptures). Bhagwaan Mahaveer is the last TEERTHANKAR of the present half-cycle of time. We are living in the TEERTH (religious order) established by Bhagwaan Mahaveer. Therefore his birth (Mahaveer Jayanti) and the day of his salvation (Mahaveer Nirvana) are celebrated.

Bhagwaan Mahaveer was born on the third day of the bright fortnight (SHUKLA PAKSHA) of the Chaitra month in the Indian calendar. Mahaveer Jayanti usually falls in the month of April. It is a very holy day for Jains. During the Mahaveer Jayanti celebration, the dreams of Mahaveer's mother, Queen Trishala, are displayed, scenes from the life of Bhagwaan Mahaveer are enacted, stories of his life are related, and the principles of Jainism are discussed.

Another important festival of Jains is Mahaveer Nirvana Day. Although the festival of lights (DIWALI or DEEPAWALI) is celebrated by most people in India, it has a special significance for Jains because they celebrate Bhagwaan Mahaveer's salvation during the festival of lights. Bhagwaan Mahaveer attained Nirvana on the last day of the dark fortnight (KRISHNA PAKSHA) of the Kaartik month in the Indian calendar. Next morning, Bhagwaan Mahaveer's principal disciple (GANADHAR), Gautam Swami attained omniscience. Diwali usually falls in the month of October. The Jain celebration includes reciting passages from scriptures, prayers, worship and discussion of the teachings of Bhagwaan Mahaveer.

The most important Jain celebration is PARYUSHAN. It is the celebration of spiritual awareness. It is celebrated for eight or ten days during the Bhadra month in the Indian calendar. PARYUSHAN is the period of intense spiritual activities. We observe partial or total fasts, study scriptures, pray and worship, listen to religious discourses, and, perform PRATIKRAMAN (careful analysis of one's past thoughts and activities—introspection). We also celebrate the ten ultimate virtues of forgiveness, modesty, sincerity, purity of spirit, truth, self-control, penance, renunciation, non-attachment and spiritual enjoyment. Thus PARYUSHAN is also called DASHALAKSHAN. At the end of PARYUSHAN, Jains celebrate the day of forgiveness (KSHAMAVANI or KSHAMAPANA). We recite the following KSHAMAPANA Sutra:

KHAAMEMI SAVVE JEEVA
SAVVE JEEVA KHAMANTU ME
METTI ME SAVVE BHUYESU
VAIRAM MAJHAM NA KENAI

I grant forgiveness to all living beings.
May all living beings grant me forgiveness.
My friendship is with all living beings.
My enmity is totally non-existent.

Jain Places Of Pilgrimage

There are many places of pilgrimage for Jains such as Sammed Shikhar, Shatrunjaya, Girinar, Pavapuri, Shravanabelgola and Mount Abu. These places are reminders of the lives of TEERTHANKARs and their salvation. They are monuments to the lofty ideals of Jainism.

In the past, many TEERTHANKARs and monks attained salvation at Sammed Shikhar and at Shatrunjaya (Palitana). Bhagwaan Neminath, the twenty-second TEERTHANKAR, attained salvation at Mount Girinar (near Junagarh, Gujarat). Bhagwaan Mahaveer attained salvation at Pavapuri (in the state of Bihar). A serene temple in the middle of a pond marks the place of TEERTHANKAR Mahaveer's Nirvana. Sammed Shikhar is in the state of Bihar. It is situated on a beautiful mountain. There are symbols of feet on the hill tops to mark the spots where the TEERTHANKARs performed pristine meditation to attain salvation. There are many beautiful temples. Shatrunjaya is also situated on a mountain, near the town of Palitana in Gujarat. There are 3500 temples on the slopes. The architecture of many of these temples is uniquely beautiful. These are some of the SIDDHA KSHETRAS (places of salvation).

Shravanbelgola in the state of Mysore has a beautiful colossal statue of Gommateshwar Bahubali. Bahubali was the son of the first TEERTHANKAR, Bhagwaan Rishabha. Bahubali also attained salvation. The statue was carved, in the tenth century A.D., out of the top of the mountain on which it stands 63 feet tall without any support.

Mount Abu is in the state of Rajasthan and it is famous for its magnificent Delwara temples. The temples are built of white marble. The marble ceilings and pillars of the temples have intricate carvings. These world famous temples are marvels of art and architecture.

Religious practices such as temple visits, pilgrimages and celebrations of spiritual aware-ness, Mahaveer Jayanti and Mahaveer Nirvana Day provide valuable spiritual experiences.

* * * * * * *

Contentment is like nectar. Those with becalmed mind are satisfied with this nectar, and they enjoy bliss. This bliss is not experienced by men who are greedy and keep running restlessly in search of wealth from here to there and from there to here.

HITOPADESH, an ancient Indian text.

* * * * * * *

Rational Conduct: Five Vows

We Jains believe that rationalism is essential for spiritual development. First we should develop rational perception and knowledge. Then we should adopt a rational conduct which conforms to rational perception and knowledge. Rationalism helps us minimize the negative influence of karma on our lives. A proper frame of mind and good conduct lead to contentment and happiness in life.

The code of conduct for Jains consists of the following five vows:

1. Non-violence (AHIMSA)
2. Truth (SATYA)
3. Non-stealing (ACHAURYA)
4. Purity of body and mind (BRAHMACHARYA)
5. Non-possessiveness (APARIGRAH)

The above code of conduct is essentially similar to the ethical code preached by other religions. Jainism, however, emphasizes that our conduct can not be rational without rational perception and knowledge. We have to be open-minded and reasonable. We have to understand the meaning and significance of our religious practices.

The Jain code of conduct is based on our concept of reality. We Jains believe that our actions should conform to our understanding and experiences. We do not believe that faith in any creed or acceptance of any superhuman personality leads to salvation. Blindly following what is written in any book or preached by an individual is not rational conduct.

68

We do not follow any moral code just because some mystical entity commands us to do so. Belief in concepts that are beyond our understanding and experience is delusion. We obtain deluding karma through such beliefs and practices. Our conduct should be proper but not because of peer pressure or fear of law. Acharya Atmaramji has written: "As animals are driven by a rod, similarly, some people behave because of law and order. However, the power of the criminal justice system does not encourage the free development of human feelings and emotions." He continues, "Peer pressure keeps people in some kind of bondage. It involves a gross tendency related to fear and desire. . . . Religion is the natural and gentle impulse of human heart."[1] The Jain religion teaches us to follow the moral code so that we can have peace and harmony in life.

The question arises: On the basis of our own understanding and experience, how can we determine what is proper conduct? The answer to this question is simple. We know that passions such as anger and greed make us unhappy. They destroy our peace of mind. We do not enjoy being hurt physically. We do not like if anyone hurts our feelings. We feel awful when we hurt the feelings of any other individual. Thoughts of violence and revenge upset us. If we have undue attachment for a toy or dress, we become unhappy when it is lost or damaged. If we learn to be content with what we have, we will enjoy real happiness in life. Our

[1] JAIN TATTVA KALIKA (Treatise On Jain Philosophy), published by Atma Gyanpitha, Mansa Mandi, Punjab, 1982, pages 8-10 of the third part.

rational conduct should be guided by these observations and experiences.

Nonviolence

Nonviolence (AHIMSA) is the foundation of the Jain outlook on life. The Jain religion teaches that all life is sacred. Every living being has a unique place in the scheme of the universe.

Acharya Umaswati has defined violence as obstruction of the life processes of self and of others effected by a lack of conscientiousness.[2] All living beings have to interact with their environment, which includes other living beings such as plants and animals. Thus violence in life is unavoidable to a certain extent. Ancient Jain thinkers classified living beings on the basis of the complexity of their life processes. The life processes of plants are simple while those of animals are highly developed. The higher the form of life, the greater the violence involved in hurting or killing it. The Jain practice of vegetarianism is based on this concept because less violence is committed in procuring and processing vegetarian foods. We Jains avoid intentional violence of all kinds. We minimize the violence towards even the plant life. Further, we remember the fact that when we commit physical and mental violence towards another living being, we have undesirable thoughts. Our own feelings are hurt in the process thus producing even more violence towards the self.

The Jain concept of nonviolence promotes peace

2 PRAMATTA YOGAAT PRAAN VYAPAROPANAM HIMSA, TATTVAARTH SUTRA, chapter 7, aphorism 13.

and harmony in society. The famous modern Jain scholar, A. N. Upadhye writes:[3]

A man of kindly temperament sheds around him an atmosphere of kindness. Jainism has firmly held that life is sacred irrespective of species, caste, color, creed or nationality. A resident of Hiroshima or Nagasaki is as sacred as one in New York or London: what his color is, what he eats, and how he dresses—these are external adjuncts. Thus, the practice of nonviolence is both an individual and a collective virtue; and this kindly attitude which requires that our hearts be free from baser impulses like anger, pride, hypocrisy, greed, envy and contempt, has a positive force and a universal appeal.

Truth and non-stealing

Truth and non-stealing are important virtues which eliminate suspicion and mistrust among individuals and create an atmosphere of security in society. We should always speak the truth. We should take only our fair share and should not indulge in any unfair business practices. We should perform our duties well, with the best of our ability. These are essential aspects of the vows of truth and non-stealing. By practicing the vows of truth and non-stealing, we will earn the trust of our fellow men. These vows promote good neighborliness and enable us to become a Jain in the true sense of the word.

---

[3] 'Mahavira And His Philosophy Of Life' included in the book Lord Mahavira And His Teachings, published by Shree Vallabhsuri Smarak Nidhi, Bombay, India, 1983.

In the article, quoted above, Dr. A. N. Upadhye writes: One's thoughts, words and acts must be consistent with each other. Further, they must create an atmosphere of confidence. A reciprocal sense of security must start with the immediate neighbor and then be gradually diffused in society at large, not only in theory but also in practice. These virtues can lead to coherent social and political groups of worthy citizens who yearn for peaceful coexistence with the well-being of the entire humanity in view.

Celibacy (BRAHMACHARYA) And Non-possessiveness (APARIGRAH):

All men have some yearning for sensual or sexual pleasure and for the acquisition of material things. However, it is a common experience that desires cause unhappiness in our lives. Thus minimizing our needs and the gradual elimination of desires are important goals in life.

One of the fundamental principles of Jainism is individual freedom. However, our freedom should not infringe on others' rights. It should not lead to problems in our lives and in society. Thus we Jains should practice celibacy. The Jain monks practice total celibacy while the householders abstain from pre-marital and extra-marital sex, and observe partial celibacy. Celibacy maintains purity of body and mind. It helps us minimize problems in life. In fact, "one-half of the U. S. teen-age population refrains from premarital sex, apparently with no mental or physical damage. The other half does not, and suffers venereal diseases, unwanted pregnancy and emotional problems. . . . . It requires no genius to know which half is better off."[4]

Non-possessiveness (APARIGRAH) is the fifth vow of Jains. It entails limiting our needs and minimizing greed. It helps us conserve energy and other natural resources. Its practice can result in social equity and justice. A highly religious person is free from possessiveness in thought, word and deed. Others practice non-possessiveness to varying degrees depending upon their stage of spiritual development.

It is observed that most problems, individually as well as collectively, arise due to indulgence in indiscriminate sensual or sexual activity and acquisitiveness. People tell lies, cheat, deceive and use unfair means on account of yearning for sensual pleasure and greed. Such practices involve violence towards self. Thus, in the final analysis, the last four vows help us minimize self-directed violence.

In conclusion, the true practice of nonviolence entails avoiding undesirable thought activity and enjoying pure thoughts and real happiness. This is rational conduct for Jains.

---

4 Kevin Barry, May 26, 1981, published in the New York Times.

* * * * * * *

Essence of humanity is knowledge, essence of knowledge is rationalism and essence of rationalism is good conduct. Remember, only good conduct gives rise to peace and equanimity.

Acharya Kundkund

* * * * * * *

㉒ A Dialogue On Vegetarianism
By Santosh C. Shah

[Shalin (5 years) shows a box of cookies to Sweta (8 years) in a grocery store.]

Shalin: Sweta, do you want to buy this box of cookies? Daddy said that we could buy some cookies.

Sweta: Yes Shalin, but we have to see the ingredients on the box because we do not eat anything containing lard, eggs or animal shortening. There are some cookies without them that we can buy.

Shalin: But many people eat meat! So why can't we?

Sweta: People who eat meat will stop eating meat when they think about and understand why no one should eat meat. We will discuss this in our Jain school (PATHSHAALA). We will buy cookies next time because we are getting late for our Jain school.

[Set up a school scene with chairs on 3 sides and Hem (13 years) as the monitor.]

Hem: What is the topic for today, Sweta?

Sweta: Today's topic is: Why should we be vegetarians? Shalin wants to understand this.

Hem: Why don't we eat meat, Shalin?

Shalin: Because we are Jains! And my mommy tells me not to eat meat.

Hem: It is good to follow our parents' instructions. Our Jain religion also teaches us that as we grow older, we will understand why we should follow these rules. Sweta, can you tell us why we do not eat meat?

Sweta: One reason is that animals are killed to get meat.

Manish (7 years): But, we don't have to kill animals and can still get meat by buying it at a restaurant.

Priya (10 years): Manish, someone else is killing them for the restaurant. That is the same as if we ourselves killed the animals. All animals want to live just as we do. They do not want to be killed just as we do not want to be killed.

Shalin: Oh yes, when we go near animals, they run away because they fear that we might hurt them.

Sejal (9 years): Right Shalin. They have the same feelings that we have. You know that in slaughter houses, animals are lined up and killed one after another.

Priya: Sejal, I can not imagine the pain of those poor animals waiting to be killed. Manish, how would we feel if a huge creature comes down from space and says, 'all people line up, I am going to kill you' ? (to be said in robot's voice)

Manish: What does the space creature say, Priya?

Everyone except Manish: ALL PEOPLE LINE UP, I AM GOING TO KILL YOU.

Manish & Shalin: It would feel horrible!!!

Priya: Those animals feel the same way.
Manish & Shalin: Now we understand.

Sweta: Besides getting bad karma by hurting the feelings of animals and killing them, there are other considerations for being a vegetarian. Man is vegetarian by nature and a vegetarian diet is better for our health.

Manish: It is also less expensive to be a vegetarian.

Anjali (11 years): You are all confusing me. Why don't we talk about one reason at a time?

Hem: Let us first take up the the point raised by Manish about meat being expensive. Even if meat, eggs and fish were less expensive than vegetarian foods, we Jains would not eat them because we believe in avoiding mental and physical violence as much as possible. However, producing meat requires a considerable amount of natural resources. It takes 16 pounds of grain and about 2500 gallons of water to produce a single pound of meat.

Manish: What are the health reasons of being a vegetarian? Don't non-vegetarian people get lots of protein and energy from meat?

Anjali: They also get lots of fat that they do not need.

Sweta: We get the same amount of energy from vegetarian food, and less fat, which is better for our health.

Sejal: The meat industry continuously talks about protein. What about it?

Hem: Recently, researchers have found that we need only about 6 to 8 percent of our daily calories to be derived from protein. Consuming high-protein (non-vegetarian) food that is rich in calories and fat is more difficult for our kidneys. It is more difficult for our kidneys to process animal proteins.

Nidhi (9 years): We get less cholesterol from our vegetarian diet, so we are less prone to suffer heart attacks.

Sejal: I heard that meat is easy to digest.

Anjali: Well, in fact, as Hem said, for humans, meat is hard to digest. The meat-eating animals have strong hydrochloric acid in their stomachs to digest meat. The acid in our stomachs is 20 times weaker than that in the stomach of a meat-eating animal. The length of our intestines is about twelve times our body length while the length of the intestines of meat-eating animals is only about three times their body length. Our teeth are different from those of meat-eating animals. Thus, man is vegetarian by nature.

Priya: I wish to add that meat eaters are also likely to consume organisms that cause diseases in animals. They also consume residues of thousands of drugs that are fed to the animals which are later killed for food.

Nidhi: You are right Priya. Meat eaters are more likely to get diseases like cancer.

Manish: It is clear that meat eating does a lot more harm to us. It is not at all good for our bodies.

Hem: Let us have Manish (15 years) and Anjali explain the religious reasons for vegetarianism.

Manish: According to Jainism, all living beings have souls. Interfering with the rights of other souls is violence. We have bad thoughts and feelings when we commit violence and thus we get bad karma.

Nidhi: How does eating meat involve violence?

Anjali: Two ways. First, eating meat involves direct or indirect physical and mental violence to animals which are killed to get meat. Second, it also results in violence of self because it is not good for our health. Also we have feelings of disregard for life when we eat non-vegetarian food, which is mental violence. Meat eating is not good for our spiritual progress.

Sejal: Is this true in the Jain religion only?

Manish: Well, all religions preach nonviolence to different extents. Jainism goes the farthest in this respect. Hinduism and Buddhism have similar concepts.

Sejal: Isn't eating plants also violence?

Manish: Some violence is involved in agriculture. However, the sense organs in plants are developed to a much lesser extent than in animals. Hence it is much less violent to obtain grains from dried up plants and to pick fruits and vegetables without destroying the entire plants.

Anjali: It should be pointed out that non-vegetarian food provides a better medium for the growth of minute living organisms (such as bacteria) than vegetarian food. Therefore, large number of minute living beings are killed in preparing and consuming non-vegetarian food. Thus vegetarianism helps us minimize violence.

Hem: Let us finish for today. We had an interesting and illuminating discussion.

References:
1. Vegetarianism In All Aspects by Preeti Yogendra Jain, Jain Study Circular, volume 8, January 1987, page 5.
2. Eating For The Eighties by Shakuntala Kothari, Jain Study Circular, volume 10, January 1989, page 19.
3. Exchange Of Ideas, Jain Study Circular, volume 10, April 1989, page 18.

* * * * * * *

There is no shortcut to life's perfection, the law of karma being inexorable. Any idea of divine grace or forgiveness is, according to Jainism, only an oversimplification of the problems of sin, suffering and redemption.

- Prof. Shri Krishna Saksena
in 'The Jain Religion'

* * * * * * *

Six Essentials

Jains are expected to fulfill their responsibility towards their family, society and country. We earn our livelihood. We make sure that our youngsters receive proper education. In earning our livelihood, our intention is always to serve other people of the society, Jains as well as non-Jains. We make sure that our gain does not become some other person's loss. We serve our country by making sure that we contribute towards the welfare of all people of the world. In addition to this, we make a sincere effort to advance on the spiritual path. For this purpose, the Jain sages have designed six essentials (AAVASHYAKs)—six activities which a Jain is expected to perform everyday. The six daily essential activities of a householder are:[1]

1. Worship of the Supreme Souls (DEV POOJA)
2. Homage to monks (GURU PAASTI)
3. Study of scriptures (SWAADHYAAYA)
4. Practice of self-control (SANYAM)
5. Penance (TAPAH)
6. Charity (DAAN).

Worship of Supreme Souls

Supreme Souls are ARIHANTs and SIDDHAs. They have either liberated themselves from the worldly cycles of birth and death (SIDDHAs) or they are well on their way to liberation (ARIHANTs). The ultimate

[1] DEV POOJA GURU PAASTIH SWAADYAAYAH SANYAMSTAPAH:
DAANAM CHETI GRIHASTHAANAM SHAT KARMAANI DINAY DINAY::

goal of all worldly souls is salvation, freedom from dependence on material objects. This dependence is caused by particles of matter called karma. These karma particles have been associated with the worldly souls since time immemorial. A worldly soul sheds some old karma and acquires some new karma continuously. This interaction between soul and karma is caused by the feelings, emotions and passions of living beings. The Supreme beings have freed themselves from the bondage of karma. Thus they have shown the path to liberation.

Worship and prayer of Supreme Souls is performed to remind us of our ultimate goal of liberation from the bondage of karma. Jains pray or worship before the images of TEERTHANKARs (the Supreme Beings) or their pictures. We can also pray to a mental image of TEERTHANKARs. We are at liberty to choose where and how we pray. Nevertheless, the procedures (VIDHIs) of prayer or worship have been outlined in religious books. Such procedures are only for the purpose of organization. They do not have any ritualistic significance since a Jain worship is not performed with the desire of any material gains.

Homage to monks

Monks are spiritually ahead of householders because they have control over their passions such as anger, pride, ego, intrigue and greed. They do not live for name and fame. They preach the teachings of Bhagwaan Mahaveer through practice.

Householders respect monks who are beyond attachment and aversion. They face honor or neglect, suffering or comfort, rich food or hunger, with equanimity. They study the scriptures and teach the principles of Jainism. They endeavor to remove delusion from the world. They do not command us to blindly follow them.

Study of Scriptures

We Jains should study the scriptures and religious books daily. We can select a religious book or article and read and discuss it with our family for fifteen minutes. Such study will go a long way towards educating our youngsters. Studying scriptures or any religious book entails understanding them and pondering over the concepts presented in them, not simply memorizing or blindly accepting them.

Self-control

We Jains should practice self-control in our daily activities as far as possible because this helps us practice nonviolence. We should minimize passions and emotions which may adversely affect our physical and mental well-being. We should avoid taking unhealthy foods. We should not speak words which may hurt others' feelings.

Penance

We Jains should perform some penance everyday. Penance can be external (physical) or internal (mental). External penance includes total fasting

(ANASHAN), partial fasting (AVAMAUDARYA), limiting requirements (VRITTI PARISAMKHYAAN), giving up delicacies (RAS PARITYAAG), sleeping in a lonely place (VIVIKTA SHAIYAASAN) and accepting inconveniences (KAAYA KLESH). Internal penance includes atonement (PRAAYASHCHITTA), reverence (VINAYA), service (VAIYAAVRITTYA), study of scriptures (SWAADHYAAYA), renunciation of pride and ego (VYUTSARG) and meditation (DHYAAN, intensive thinking about the nature of reality).

Charity

In Jain scriptures, charity (DAAN) is defined as self-sacrifice. It consists of giving food (AAHAAR), medicine (AUSHADHI), education (SHASTRA) and freedom from fear (ABHAYA). Charity should be performed with pure thoughts, "not in the sense where the giver is superior to the receiver; both are equal. If there is any idea of superiority, it encourages or feeds pride. Pride obscures knowledge."[2]

Some religious books have described the following six essentials:

1. Equanimity (SAAMMAAIYAM or SAAMAAYIK)
2. Obeisance to twenty-four TEERTHANKARS (CHAUVEESATTHAO)
3. Homage (VANDANYAM)
4. Introspection (PADIKKAMANAM or PRATIKRAMAN)
5. Regulating the activities of body, speech and mind (KAAUSSAGG)
6. Determination (PACHCHAKHAAN or PRATYAAKHYAAN)

2 Herbert Warren's Jainism, page 90.

These are similar to the six essentials outlined earlier[3]. We should understand that the names or the order of the six essentials is not important. What is important is to have pure thoughts while practicing the six essentials. Proper practice of six essentials improves our knowledge and understanding of the principles of the Jain religion. It leads to shedding or transformation of undesirable karma. It makes us better individuals. It helps us improve our physical and mental health. This is what being a Jain is all about.

Bibliography:

Herbert Warren's Jainism (based chiefly on talks and lectures by Virchand R. Gandhi), published by Vallabhsuri Smarak Nidhi Publication, Bombay.

Jain Dharm Shikshavali (Hindi), Part 4, by Pandit Ugra Sen Jain, published by A. B. D. Jain Parishad Publishing House, Delhi.

Jaina Darshan (Gujarati) by Muni Shri Nyayavijayji.

---

[3] Herbert Warren's Jainism, pages 88-89.

* * * * * * *

So long as there is desire or want, it is a sure sign that there is imperfection. A perfect free being cannot have any desire. God cannot want anything. If He desires, He cannot be God. He will be imperfect. So all the talk about God desiring this and that, and becoming angry and pleased by turns, is baby talk but means nothing. Therefore, it has been taught by all teachers: Desire nothing, give up all desires and be perfectly satisfied.

Swami Vivekanand

* * * * * * *

Alphabet Of Jain Principles

Compiled by Duli Chandra & Sunita Jain

A. A is for ARIHANTs.
ARIHANTs are supreme human beings who devote their entire lives to the uplift of life on earth.

A is for ACHARYAS.
ACHARYAS are the sages who master the principles of religion and preach them.

A is for ANEKAANTAVAAD.
ANEKAANTAVAAD is multiplicity of viewpoints. We should try to understand the viewpoints of other people also.

B. B is for blind faith.
Blind faith is delusion (misconception). It does not lead to salvation.

C. C is for character.
Remember that if wealth is lost, nothing is lost; if health is lost, something is lost; and, if character is lost, everything is lost.

C is for celibacy (BRAHMACHARYA).
Celibacy helps us maintain purity of body and mind.

C is for compassion.
Compassion is an important virtue.

D. D is for deluding karma.

The deluding (MOHANEEYA) karma may prevent us from having a proper outlook and from understanding reality.

D is for drinking and drugs.
We must avoid drinking and drugs because they affect our ability to judge right and wrong.

E. E is for eight kinds of karma. They are:
1. Perception-obscuring karma
2. Knowledge-obscuring karma
3. Feeling-producing karma
4. Deluding karma
5. Life-span-determining karma
6. Physique-determining karma
7. Status-determining karma
8. Obstructing karma

F. F is for forgiveness.
We should forgive others. We should not take revenge.

F is for feeling-producing karma.
The feeling-producing (VEDANEEYA) karma is responsible for our feelings of pleasure and pain.

G. G is for God.
Each pure soul (SIDDHA), free from the bondage of all material particles, is God. SIDDHAs do not interfere in the events of the universe.

G is for GANADHAR.
GANADHARs are disciples of TEERTHANKARs. They acquire the knowledge of the principles of

religion from TEERTHANKARs and explain it to the masses. They compose the scriptures. They are the exponents of the teachings of TEERTHANKARs.

H. H is for help.
According to the principles of Jainism, the worldly living beings help each other.

I. I is for independence.
Each individual soul is independent.

I is for identity.
We should keep our identity.

J. J is for JIN (victor).
JINs are the victors who have conquered their passions. JINs are beyond attachment and aversion (VEETARAAG).

K. K is for karma.
Karmas are very fine particles of matter attached to the worldly souls. Karma may affect our lives. Living beings can modify the influence of karma on their lives.

K is for knowledge-obscuring karma.
The knowledge-obscuring (JNAANAAVARNI) karma may prevent us from obtaining proper knowledge.

K is for KSHAMAAPANA (KSHAMAVANI).
On the last day of the celebration of spiritual awareness, we observe KSHAMAAPANA (KSHAMAVANI) and ask forgiveness from all.

L. L is for limiting our possessions.

It is called APARIGRAH. It helps us minimize greed and conserve natural resources.

L is for life-span-determining karma.
The life-span-determining (AAYU) karma determines the maximum life-span of a living being.

M. M is for MOKSHA.
When a worldly soul frees itself from the bondage of karma, it attains MOKSHA or NIRVANA (salvation).

N. N is for nonviolence.
Nonviolence (AHIMSA) is the supreme religion. It gives us peace of mind.

O. O is for Omniscient.
A person who knows the absolute truth is Omniscient. When a soul frees itself from perception-obscuring, knowledge-obscuring, deluding and obstructing karma, it becomes Omniscient (KEVALI).

P. P is for penance.
Penance (TAPAH) is willed (voluntary) elimination of ego and desires.

P is for perception-obscuring karma.
The perception-obscuring (DARSHANAAVARNI) karma may prevent the soul from developing proper perception.

Q. Q is for quiet.
Close your eyes, have good thoughts and make a

determination to do good deeds. This is meditation. It gives peace of mind.

R. R is for religion.
Religion is the science of living. Religion leads to peace of mind and happiness in life.

R is for rationalism.
Do not accept or adopt anything just because it is written or preached. Accept what seems reasonable. This is known as SAMYAKTVA in Jainism.

R is for relativism (SYAADAVAAD).
We should learn to look at things from different viewpoints. What is right for us may not be right for others.

S. S is for soul.
Soul makes the difference between the living beings and non-living objects. All living beings of the world have souls while the inanimate objects do not.

S is for SIDDHA.
SIDDHAs are supreme beings who have absolute perception, knowledge and bliss. SIDDHAs are souls that have attained NIRVANA.

S is for SADHU.
SADHUs are sages who devote their lives to the selfless pursuit of enlightenment of all.

S is for status-determining karma.
The status-determining (GOTRA) karma deter-

mines our family status (position in society).

T. T is for TEERTHANKAR.
A TEERTHANKAR reinstates the religious order. There have been 24 TEERTHANKARs in the present half-cycle of time. Mahaveer is the twenty-fourth TEERTHANKAR.

T is for truth.
Speaking the truth gives us peace of mind.

T is for the three jewels of Jainism.
The three jewels (RATNATRAYA) are proper (rational) perception, proper knowledge and proper conduct. These lead to salvation.

U. U is for UPAADHYAAYA.
UPAADHYAAYAs are sages who study and enhance their knowledge of matter and souls.

V. V is for victor (JIN).
JINs are the true victors. They conquer their passions and have control over their senses.

V is for VEETARAAG.
VEETARAAG JINs have no attachment (RAAG) and aversion (DWESH).

V is for vegetarianism.
A vegetarian diet not only promotes nonviolence but it is also good for our physical and mental well-being.

W. W is for worship.
We worship the virtues such as non-attachment,

absence of desires and omniscience. We worship the images of TEERTHANKARs as symbols of their virtues.

X. X is for x-rays.
Our perception should be deep and penetrating like x-rays.

Y. Y is for YOGA.
YOGA is the activity of body, speech and mind. Our physical and mental activities should be nonviolent. This will lead to good health, happiness and peace of mind. This is the true practice of YOGA according to Jainism.

Z. Z is for zeal.
In the zeal for practicing our religion, we should not hurt others' feelings. We should tolerate others' views and respect other religions.

* * * * * * *

People will not judge us by the creed we profess, or the slogans we shout, but by our work, sacrifice, honesty and purity of character. - Mahatma Gandhi

* * * * * * *